BOOK 3

the POINTER SYSTEM

for the

Piano

A Fast, Easy and Direct Approach to the Learning of Chords and Melodies on the Piano

HAL•LEONARD® CORPORATION

7777 W. BLUEMOUND RD. P.O. BOX 13819 MILWAUKEE, WI 53213

TABLE OF CONTENTS

SONGS

In Books 1 and 2 of the Pointer System for Piano you learned seven of the more commonly used major chords and how to form minor, seventh, sixth, augmented and diminished chords from these basic chords.

Diagramed below are the remaining five major chords (there are twelve major chords altogether).

Learn these chords thoroughly. Refer to the "Pointer Chord Rules" for forming the variations of them.

B CHORD
Trademark

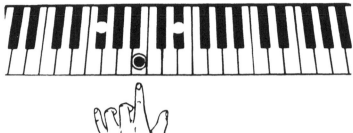

Eb CHORD
Trademark

Ab CHORD
Trademark

Db CHORD
Trademark

Gb CHORD
Trademark

4

You have played songs written in the Keys of C Major and F Major. Now let's play in another key----the Key of G Major.

Again, the melodies and chords of songs written in the Key of G will be built around the G Major Scale. Let's play this scale to get the "feel" of the new key.

To maintain the major scale pattern you will play F♯

"I've Been Working On The Railroad" is written in the Key of G Major. The sharp placed at the beginning of the staff on the fifth line (the F line) is the **key signature** and indicates that all F's are to be played as F♯ (F sharp).

CHORDS USED IN THIS SONG:

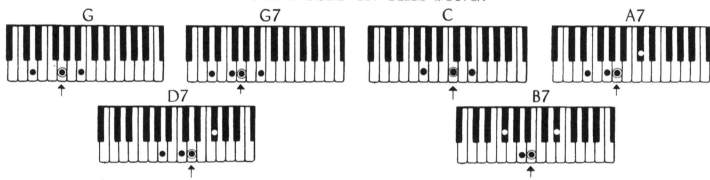

I'VE BEEN WORKING ON THE RAILROAD

CHORDS USED IN THIS SONG:

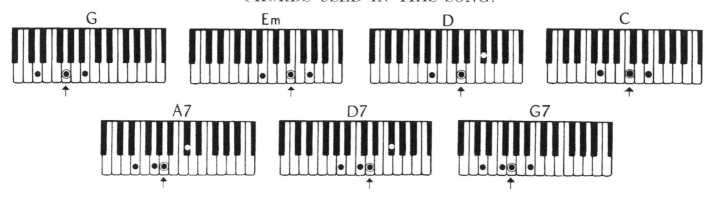

HOLY, HOLY, HOLY!

J. B. Dykes

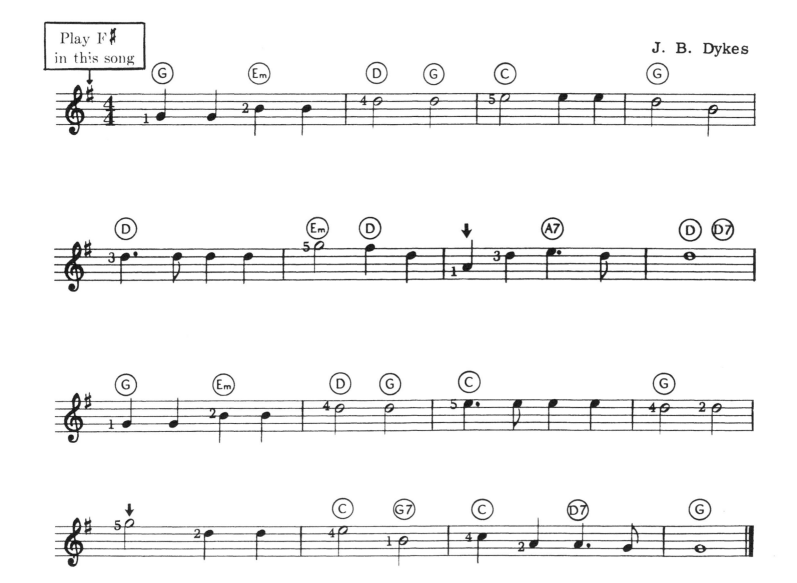

In Book 2 you played rhythm in 3. Now you will learn to play another basic rhythm used in music--"RHYTHM IN 4" It is characterized by a series of **four** rhythmic beats with the emphasis or **accent** on **beat no. 1** and **beat no. 3**.

> **THE BASIC RHYTHM IN 4 IS USED FOR SONGS WITH THE FOLLOWING TIME SIGNATURES:** 2/4 and 4/4.

A common expression for rhythm in 4 is:

OOM-pa   OOM-pa   OOM-pa   OOM-pa

You will play **bass notes** on counts 1 and 3 and **chords** on counts 2 and 4.

The playing pattern will be as follows:

On Beat 1------Play the chord name note as a bass note.

On Beat 2------Play the Pointer Chord and release immediately.

On Beat 3------Same as Beat 1.

On Beat 4------Same as Beat 2.

The playing pattern is illustrated below:
Again the quarter note (♩) indicates the **bass** and the smaller quarter note (♩) indicates the **chord**.

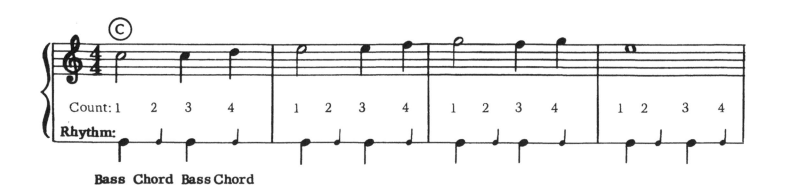

Now play the following songs using rhythm in 4.

Below are two rhythm patterns occuring in "Oh Susanna". Study them carefully before playing the song.

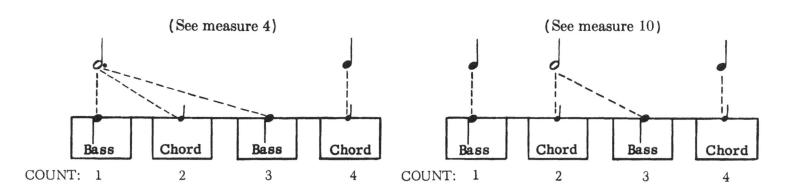

(See measure 4)

Bass	Chord	Bass	Chord
COUNT: 1 2 3 4

(See measure 10)

Bass	Chord	Bass	Chord
COUNT: 1 2 3 4

Remember the importance of playing the rhythm part separately before adding the melody.

 Do not use the sustaining pedal until you have more experience in playing rhythm in 4.

CHORDS USED IN THIS SONG:

C   G7   F

OH SUSANNA

Stephen Foster

Rhythm:

Bass Chord Bass Chord

(continue rhythm as above)

Study the rhythm pattern below before playing "Camptown Races"

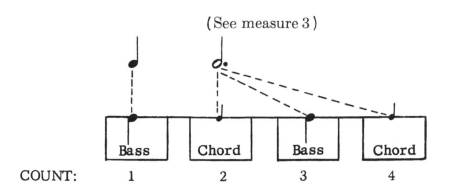

(See measure 3)

COUNT: 1   2   3   4

CHORDS USED IN THIS SONG:

CAMPTOWN RACES

Stephen Foster

Play F♯ in this song.

Rhythm:

(continue rhythm)

Use the sustaining pedal for the next song. Follow this procedure:

1. Depress the sustaining pedal as you play the bass note (Count 1).
2. Release and again depress the sustaining pedal as you play the **next** bass note (Count 3).

CHORDS USED IN THIS SONG:

MARINE HYMN

The rhythm pattern of a **dotted quarter** followed by an **eighth** note is found in "Good Night Ladies". (See measure 7). The **bass note** and **first chord** are played with the dotted quarter note; the eighth note (or "and" of the second count) is played after the **first chord** ---The same playing pattern repeats for counts 3 and 4.

LIKE THIS:

(See measure 7)

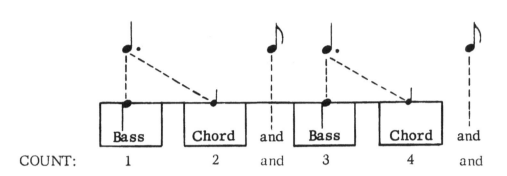

CHORDS USED IN THIS SONG:

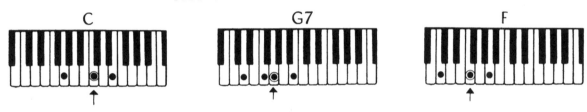

GOOD NIGHT LADIES

Traditional

CHORDS USED IN THIS SONG:

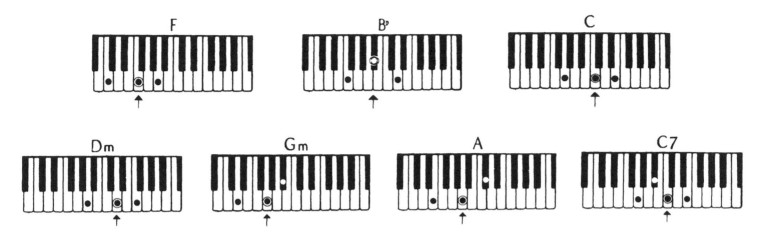

ANNIE LAURIE

Lady John Scott

Play Bb in this song.

One of the most important studies on any musical instrument is the study of scales. Scale studies serve several purposes: They develop finger technique and facility and increase your basic understanding of how music is constructed. They also develop your sense of tonal feeling.

FIRST----let us study the **C Major Scale.** This is the natural scale, played entirely on the white keys. Start on Middle C and play all the white keys up to the next C. The fingering is marked on the keyboard diagram below:

C D E F G A B C

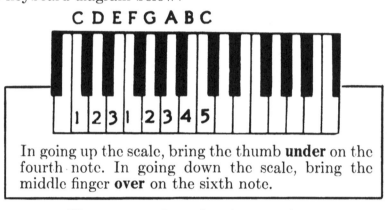

In going up the scale, bring the thumb **under** on the fourth note. In going down the scale, bring the middle finger **over** on the sixth note.

The correct fingering is very important. Learn it thoroughly and practice it until you develop speed both playing **up** and **down. Use reverse fingering coming down the scale.**

The **C Major Scale** is constructed on a certain pattern of whole steps and half steps. You learned in Book 2 that a **half step** is the distance from one key to the very next key and a **whole step** is two half steps.

HERE IS THE PATTERN OF WHOLE AND HALF STEPS IN THE C MAJOR SCALE.

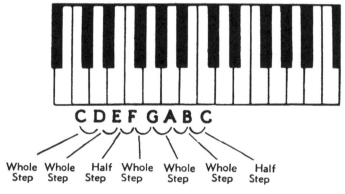

If we number the notes of the scale, 1 through 8, we find that there is a half step between 3 and 4 and between 7 and 8.

> **All Major Scales are built the same way----whole steps** between all notes **except** 3 and 4, and 7 and 8.

Now, build a major scale starting on G. Use the same fingering as in the C Scale remembering that there are whole steps between all notes except 3 and 4, and 7 and 8. **Now,** see if you have played it as in the diagram below. You will find that in order to maintain the pattern of whole and half steps, it is necessary to use the black key---F♯ .

G MAJOR SCALE

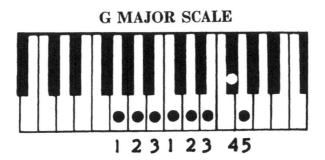

1 2 3 1 2 3 4 5

Major scales built on the white keys----C, D, E, G, A, B----all use the same fingering: 1, 2, 3, 1, 2, 3, 4, 5.

A major scale can be built on any note of the keyboard and is named for the note on which it starts.

NOW BUILD THE MAJOR SCALES BELOW

E MAJOR SCALE

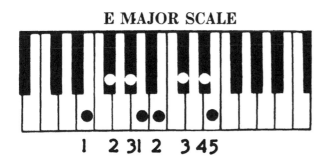

1 2 31 2 3 4 5

D MAJOR SCALE

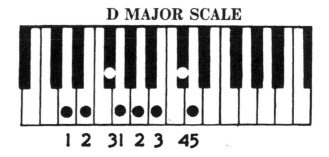

1 2 31 2 3 4 5

A MAJOR SCALE

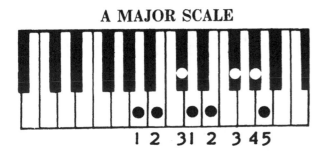

1 2 31 2 3 4 5

B MAJOR SCALE

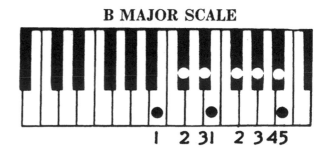

1 2 31 2 3 4 5

 Set a goal of learning two scales each week. Soon you will know them all. Later we will study the major scales built on the black keys.

The rhythm of a **dotted quarter** followed by an **eighth** note is presented in "L'Estudiantina" (See measure 8). The **bass note** is played with the first quarter note; **both chords** are played with the dotted quarter; the eighth note (or "and" of the third count) is played after the second chord----

LIKE THIS:

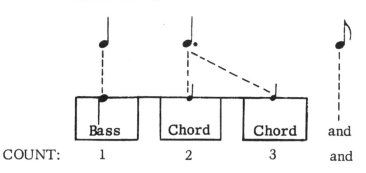

CHORDS USED IN THIS SONG:

L' ESTUDIANTINA

E. Waldteufel

CHORDS USED IN THIS SONG:

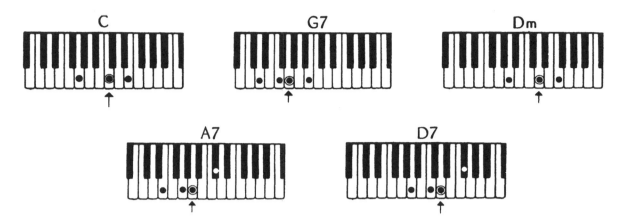

AFTER THE BALL

Charles K. Harris

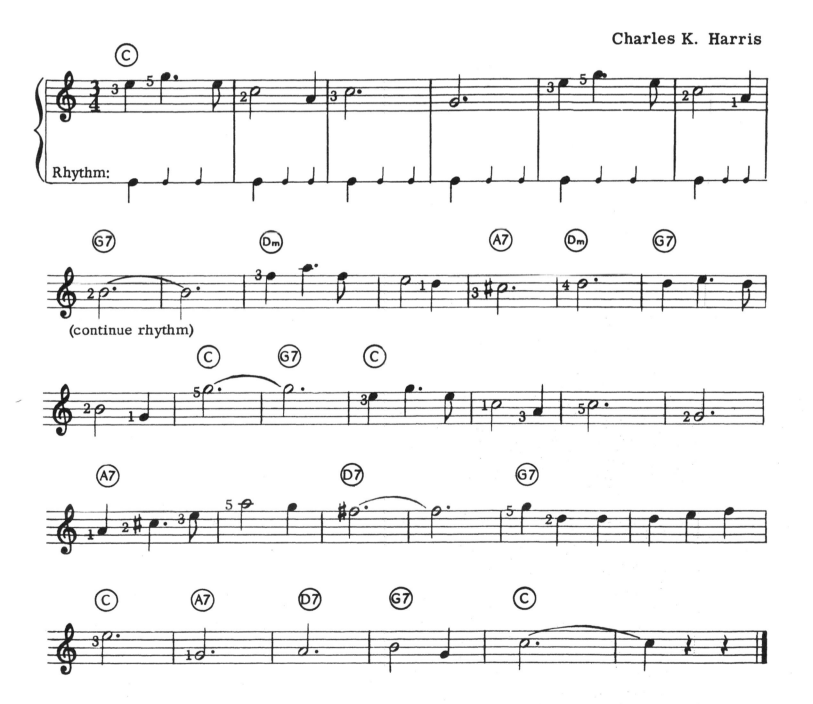

You will find many of your favorite selections in the songs that follow. ALWAYS COUNT!!!!

You will also find in these songs a rhythm pattern which you have not played----this is the pattern of two or more **eighth notes** played in succession. **Remember**----The **second** eighth note or **"and"** is played after the bass or chord has been struck.
Study the examples given below:

CHORDS USED IN THIS SONG:

SANTA LUCIA

Traditional

CHORDS USED IN THIS SONG:

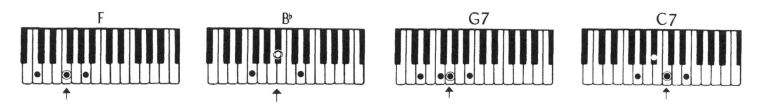

IN THE GOOD OLD SUMMERTIME

CHORDS USED IN THIS SONG:

HOME ON THE RANGE

Traditional

CHORDS USED IN THIS SONG:

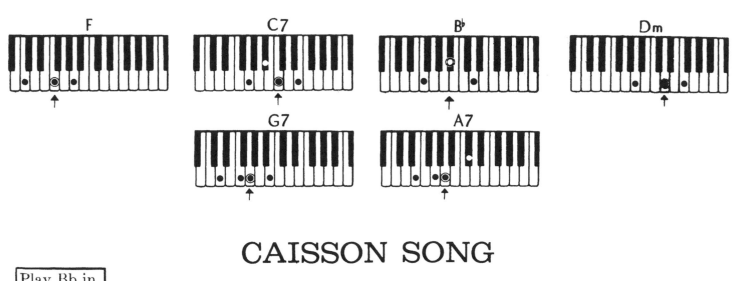

CAISSON SONG

20

CHORDS USED IN THIS SONG:

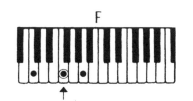
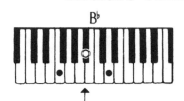
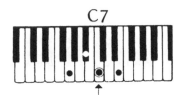
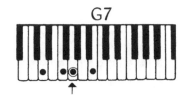

MY WILD IRISH ROSE

CHORDS USED IN THIS SONG:

MINUTE WALTZ

F. Chopin

Remember that all major scales are built the same way:

---Eight notes in every major scale.

----Whole steps between each note except 3 and 4, and 7 and 8.

To determine the correct fingering on major scales built on the **black keys:**

----Start all scales with the second finger.

----Bring the thumb under when going from a black key to a white key.

Gb (F♯) MAJOR SCALE

Ab (G♯) MAJOR SCALE

Db (C♯) MAJOR SCALE

Eb (D♯) MAJOR SCALE

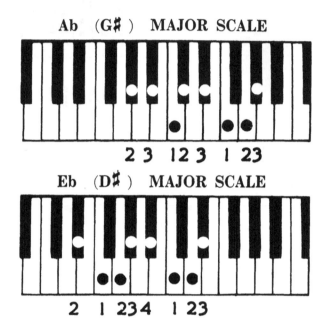

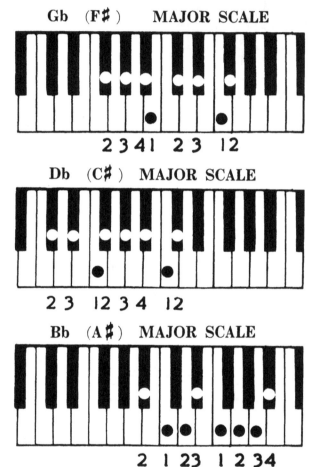

Bb (A♯) MAJOR SCALE

The fingering of all major scales built on black keys is started with the second finger. Bring the thumb under when going from a black key to a white key. Come down the scale with reverse fingering.

You have now built major scales on every note except F. This is the only scale which does not use either of the preceding fingering patterns.

Here is the fingering of the F Major Scale.

F MAJOR SCALE

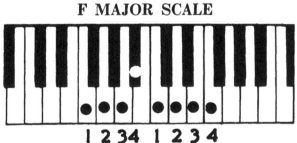

Practice the major scales diligently and often. Become so familiar with them that you can play any one of them rapidly and easily. **Remember this practice hint**------Set the goal of learning **two** scales each week. When you know all of them, continue to review at each practice period.

CHORDS USED IN THIS SONG:

GOLD AND SILVER WALTZ

Franz Lehar

Play F♯ in this song.

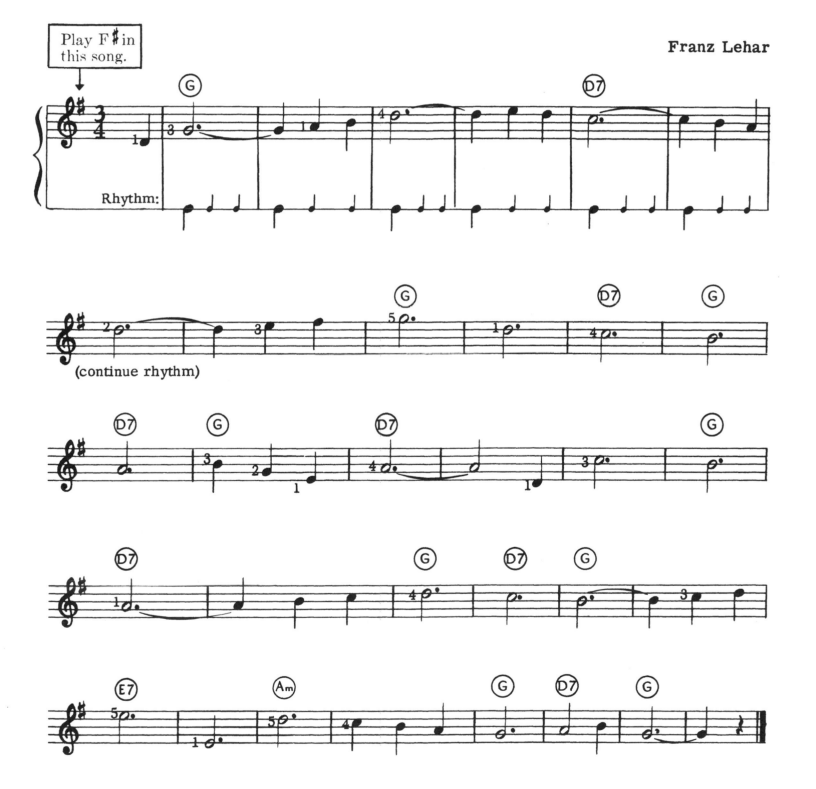

Rhythm:

(continue rhythm)

CHORDS USED IN THIS SONG:

LIEBESTRAUM

F. Liszt

CHORDS USED IN THIS SONG:

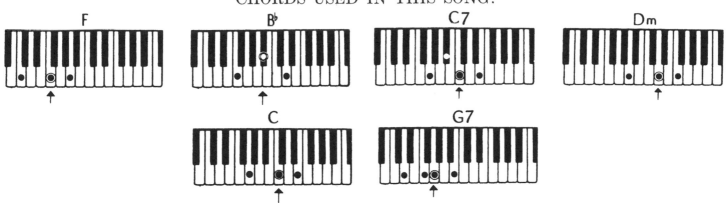

WHISPERING HOPE

Alice Hawthorne

Here is the first of the "KEYBOARD POINTERS" which will help to increase your finger facility.

You have already played the C, F and G Major Scales. Often scales or parts of scales will be used in a melody line. The "Keyboard Pointers" below will illustrate the kind of scale forms you may find in songs written in the Key of C.

To begin play evenly and slowly. Then gradually work up speed.

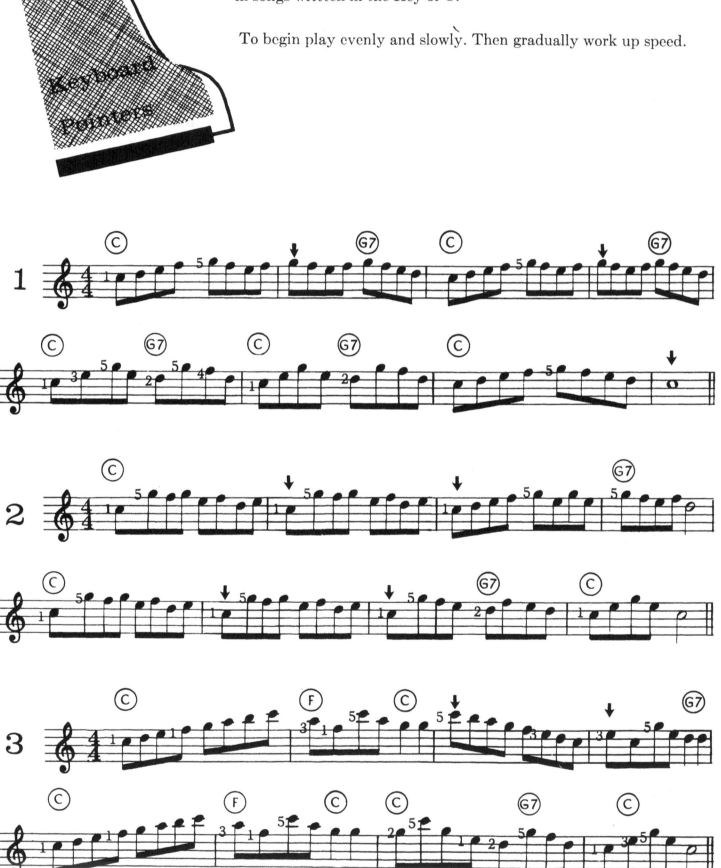

CHORDS USED IN THIS SONG:

JINGLE BELLS

Rythm:

(continue rhythm)

CHORDS USED IN THIS SONG:

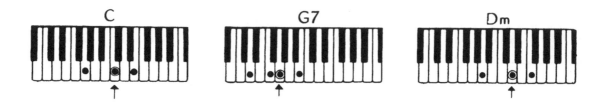

VIENNA LIFE WALTZ

Johann Strauss

You will find many of your favorite songs in the POINTER SYSTEM series of SUP-PLEMENTARY BOOKS FOR PIANO. See the back cover of this book for a complete listing.